To Hannah, who exemplifies the beautiful *"**Heart of a Caregiver**"...*

    The Light within you makes a difference in every life you touch!

To Anita, whose precious Servant's heart was a pattern for this book . . .

    The care you give to others reflects the very Heart of God!

To Liz, who was the original inspiration for the title poem . . .

    Thank you for giving such loving care to my grandmother!

HEART
of a
CAREGIVER

Touching Lives with Compassion and Care

PAULA J. FOX

"Every day thousands of unsung heroes bring **CARING** and compassion to the lives of millions. Their names are never featured in the headlines, but our world would be a much darker place without them."

— Charles Devlin

Table of Contents

Introduction

Most of us at some point in our lives experience what it's like to be a *Caregiver* for a limited time. . . caring for a small child or a family member who is either sick or is recovering from an accident or surgery, or helping with the care of an aging or disabled loved one. During such times we begin to understand the physical demands and emotional strains related to the constant *CARE* of another individual.

It helps us gain valuable insight into the level of patience, compassion and dedication required from the special people who make the *choice* to commit their lives in *service* to those who are hurting, to those who need comfort and encouragement and to those who need compassionate loving care 24/7.

This book is written as a tribute to all of those with the ***Heart of a Caregiver,*** those who have made the choice to serve others and to be a *"healing presence"* in our world. . . the professionals in the healthcare field . . . the nurses, CNAs, and other personnel in hospitals, nursing homes, assisted living facilities, hospice care, etc. . . . . as well as the multitude of husbands, wives, adult children and others who find themselves in a position of *CARING* for loved ones in their homes.

The hours are long and exhausting. The work is hard and never-ending, and there is personal pain and sacrifice involved in *CARING*. This is where true ***Heroes*** are found.

"True heroism is not the urge to surpass all others at whatever cost,
but the urge to SERVE others at whatever cost."
— Arthur Ashe

There is nothing to compare with the *Beauty* and *Significance* of this *HEART* that ***gives*** so unselfishly in service to others.

If you are a *Caregiver . . .* ***Thank you for making a difference*** in the lives you touch.

"To make a difference is not a matter of accident . . .
People **CHOOSE** *to make a difference."*

— Maya Angelou

THE HEART OF A CAREGIVER

by Paula J. Fox

In the world of pain and suffering,
true *heroes* can be found . . .
providing special comfort and relief.

They *choose* to make a difference,
regardless of the cost . . .
always willing to help others in their grief.

It's hard to persevere at times
A ***Caregiver's*** job is *tough!*
It takes extra strength and courage to get through.

But God designed a ***HEART*** for them
to handle every challenge . . .
so they *can DO* what others *cannot do.*

He made this ***HEART*** much *STRONGER*
just to handle all the weight . . .
of the many heavy burdens it must bear.

And He covered it with *SOFTNESS*
to help cushion all the hurt . . .
with *Empathy* and tender loving *Care*.

He also made it *FLEXIBLE*
to bend but not to break . . .
when things don't always go the way they're planned.

And it had to be *SELF-HEALING*
when hurtful things are said . . .
by those who just don't seem to understand.

He gave it more *RESILIENCE*
to bounce back and not get crushed . . .
when disappointment battles against hope.

And He knew a *SENSE OF HUMOR*
would be needed every day . . .
to give laughter and provide the strength to cope.

He made it with a battery
that never does run down . . .
for a *Caregiver's* day will never end.

It just keeps going . . . and keeps going,
always one more thing to do . . .
with another crisis just around the bend.

And of course, this *HEART*'s an upgrade
in so many other ways . . .
He made it *Kinder* . . . more *Unselfish* than the rest.

With more *Patience* . . . and *Compassion*
and a *Love* that never ends.
Compared to all the others . . .

it's the BEST!

"After the verb 'To Love'…
'To Help'
is the most beautiful verb
in the world."

— Bertha von Suttner

Humility

. . . is the **Core Quality** in the *HEART of a Caregiver,* the natural inclination to consider others first, and to want what's best for them.

The one who chooses this life of *Serving* and *Caring* for others follows the example of Mother Teresa, who was admired by the world and served the poorest of the poor . . . not with a "poor me" attitude . . . but with great *Dignity* and *Joy.*

If you are a *Caregiver,* you too have this beautiful **Servant's Heart**. Your deep desire to help others is at the core of your being and defines who you are. Instead of focusing on yourself, you are focused on the needs of those around you and are always looking for ways to help.

Sometimes the patients you serve are easy to love and bring you joy. Other times, you may be called upon to help those who are *difficult* and have no appreciation for the service you give. Those patients are often the ones who *need you the most.*

As a *Caregiver,* you are up to this challenge because you have chosen a life of **Giving** . . . a life of **Serving** . . . a life of **Loving** even the unlovable. You have a Heart that **CARES.**

"Serving others
is not a job for the weak.
It takes individuals with

great STRENGTH, fortitude
and self-sacrifice to wear the
garment of Humility. That's why we
call them HEROES."

— Paula J. Fox

His name was Jason, and he was about six foot five with a powerful presence but a gentle countenance. He had been a nurse for 15 years, and there was a definite difference about him . . . a level of compassion and care that was above the norm.

The thing that stands out in my mind is the way he demonstrated a sensitive servant's heart every time he walked into the room with a PAUSE to deliberately acknowledge the patient as a person of value. This simple act spoke volumes.

I wrote this poem as a tribute to all the "Jasons" in the world, both male and female, who give such compassionate care!

A SERVANT'S HEART

by Paula J. Fox

With his long blonde hair in a ponytail
he was muscular and tall.
When he first walked in, he just didn't fit
my image of a *Nurse* at all

But this gentle giant had a ***Servant's HEART***
and I soon began to see
He was a picture of compassion and kindness
and as skilled as a *Nurse* could be

There was something special about his manner
that showed dignity and respect
He cared for the person *inside* the body
with a heart and a soul to protect

He entered the room which was sterile and *cold*
but he brought in a ***warmth*** with him
Introducing himself, he smiled at his patient
and *PAUSED* before he began

He called her by name and looked in her eyes
taking time to really *see*
beyond what was wrong with her physical body
to what other needs there might be

As he *PAUSED*, he folded his hands together
leaning forward as if to say
(with a very slight bow in his body language)
"I'm here to **SERVE** you today"

He took a minute to ***listen*** to her
allowing her voice to be heard
validating her worth as a person
giving *Strength* without saying a word

I watched what transpired in that moment of time
as he gave her his focused ***attention***
Expressing such genuine care and concern
he relieved her apprehension

I could see her heart begin to relax
when she knew she could trust in his *CARE*
He eased her mind with his comforting presence
in the very brief time he was there

What a special lesson I learned that day
from this kind and compassionate *Heart*.
Just a simple *PAUSE* . . . to show you care
makes *Nursing* a beautiful *ART*!

"Nursing is an Art ...

And if it is to be made an Art, it requires
an exclusive devotion as hard a preparation
as any painter's or sculptor's work.

For what is having to do with dead canvas
or dead marble, compared with having to do with
the living body, the temple of God's spirit?

It is one of the Fine Arts ...

I had almost said ...

The Finest of Fine Arts."

—Florence Nightingale

ALL ARE SIGNIFICANT

by Joann C. Jones

During my second year of nursing school our professor gave us a quiz. I breezed through the questions until I read the last one . . .

"What is the first name of the woman who cleans the school?"

Surely this was a joke. I had seen the cleaning woman several times, but how would I know her name? I handed in my paper, leaving the last question blank. Before the class ended, one student asked if the last question would count toward our grade.

"Absolutely!" the professor said. *"In your careers, you will meet many people. **ALL are Significant!** They deserve your ATTENTION and CARE, even if all you do is smile and say hello."*

I've never forgotten that lesson. I also learned her name was Dorothy.

"Give everyone you meet the Triple-A Treatment:
Attention, Affirmation, Appreciation."

— John C. Maxwell

"There are two types of people . . .

those who come into a room and say,
'Well, here I am!'

and those who come in and say,
'Ah, there you are!'"

—Frederick L. Collins

WHEN GOD CREATED NURSES...

Author Unknown

When the Lord made *NURSES*, He was into his sixth day of overtime. An angel appeared and said, *"You're doing a lot of fiddling around on this one."* And the Lord said, *"Have you read the specs on this order?*

"A NURSE has to be able to help an injured person, breathe life into a dying person, and give comfort to a family that has lost their only child . . . and not wrinkle their uniform.

"They have to be able to lift three times their own weight, work 12 to 16 hours straight without missing a detail, console a grieving mother as they are doing CPR on a baby they know will never breathe again.

"They have to be in top mental condition at all times, running on too-little sleep, black coffee and half-eaten meals. And they have to have six pairs of hands."

The angel shook her head slowly and said, *"Six pairs of hands . . . no way!"*

"It's not the hands that are causing me problems," said the Lord, *"It's the two pairs of eyes a NURSE has to have."*

"That's on the standard model?" asked the angel.

The Lord nodded. *"One pair that does quick glances while making note of any physical changes . . . and another pair of eyes that can look with empathy on the patient who is hurting and say, "I'm so sorry you're in pain, but I'll be right here for you."*

"Lord," said the angel, touching his sleeve, *"rest and work on this tomorrow."*

"I can't," said the Lord, *"I already have a model that can talk to a 250-pound grieving family member whose child has been hit by a drunk driver (who, by the way, is laying in the next room uninjured) . . . and feed a family of five on a nurse's paycheck."*

The angel circled the model of the *NURSE* very slowly . . . *"Can it think?"* she asked.

"You bet," said the Lord. *"It can tell you the symptoms of 100 illnesses; recite drug calculations in its sleep; intubate, defibrillate, medicate, and continue CPR nonstop until help arrives . . . and still it keeps its sense of humor.*

"NURSES must also have phenomenal personal control. They have to be able to deal with a multi-victim trauma, coax a frightened elderly person to unlock their door, comfort a murder victim's family . . . and then read in the daily paper how NURSES are insensitive and uncaring and are only doing a job."

Finally, the angel bent over and ran her finger across the cheek of the *NURSE. "There's a leak,"* she pronounced. *"I told you that you were trying to put too much into this model."*

"That's not a leak," said the Lord, ***"It's a tear."***

"What's the tear for?" asked the angel.

*"It's for the times when it hurts to be a NURSE . . . for the **pain** of a Caring Heart that aches for a patient that can't be cured, or cries with the one who has experienced loss. It's for the heartache of trying in vain to save a patient who dies.*

*"But it's also a tear of **joy** for the times when miracles happen . . . and for the times when being a NURSE means making a real difference in someone's life."*

"You're a genius," said the angel.

The Lord looked somber. *"I didn't put it there,"* He said.
"It comes from the HEART."

"To **do** what nobody else will do . . .
in a **way** that nobody else can do . . .
in **spite** of all that we go through . . .
is to be a **NURSE**."

—RAWSI WILLIAMS RN, BSN, CQRMS-LTC

"Our job as Nurses is to cushion the sorrow and celebrate the joy while we are just 'doing our jobs.'"

— Christine Belle, RN, BSN

Empathy

. . . is the **Chord of Love** found deep within the *HEART of a Caregiver* . . . capable of reaching out and wrapping itself around the heart of another in a psychological hug.

Sympathy is the sweet expression of care and concern for another, but *Empathy* enables you to truly connect *heart to heart* with those who are hurting . . . sharing their pain and sorrow by putting yourself in their place, opening your *Heart* to see and hear what they are going through, and conveying that you understand how they *feel*.

Pain is universal. No life is free from pain, and you know from experience that it not only hurts, but it can affect behavior, sometimes making people rude and irrational . . . demanding immediate attention and relief. It can totally incapacitate and exhaust both physically and emotionally.

With a *Heart* that **CARES**, you are sensitive to other people's *feelings and emotions* . . . and you offer them understanding, support and comfort by empathizing with your *body language* as well as your words.

"Our patients will know what's in our HEART from the expression that's on our face . . . By sharing their face, we will share their heart."

— Scott Louis Diering, M.D.

SEEING THROUGH THE EYES OF YOUR HEART

by Paula J. Fox

In the field of healthcare, there are battles raging everywhere as patients struggle against fear, pain, loss, and heartache. The quote, *"Be kinder than necessary, for everyone you meet is fighting some sort of battle"* is especially appropriate in these situations.

When people are hurting, they often act out in irregular ways, but the *Heart of a Caregiver* is able to look beyond their behavior and offer them kindness and support in the midst of their battle.

In his book, *The 7 Habits of Highly Effective People*, Stephen Covey writes about an experience he had on a subway in New York which beautifully illustrates the importance of looking on these people with empathy . . . ***seeing through the eyes of your HEART***.

He describes what he calls a "paradigm shift" . . . that moment when he suddenly had a new perspective and was able to *"see"* things differently . . . that moment when *Empathy* emerged . . .

People were sitting quietly, some reading newspapers, some lost in thought, some resting with their eyes closed. It was a calm, peaceful scene. Then suddenly, a man and his children entered the subway car. The children were so loud and rambunctious that instantly the whole climate changed.

The man sat down next to me and closed his eyes, apparently oblivious to the situation. The children were yelling back and forth, throwing things, even grabbing people's papers. It was very disturbing. And yet, the man sitting next to me did nothing.

It was difficult not to feel irritated. I could not believe that he could be so insensitive as to let his children run wild like that and do nothing about it, taking no responsibility at all. It was easy to see that everyone else on the subway felt irritated too.

"Could a greater **miracle** take place than for us to look through each other's eyes for an instant?"

— Henry David Thoreau

So finally, with what I felt was unusual patience and restraint, I turned to him and said, *"Sir, your children are really disturbing a lot of people. I wonder if you couldn't control them a little more?"*

The man lifted his gaze as if to come to a consciousness of the situation for the first time and said softly, *"Oh, you're right. I guess I should do something about it. We just came from the hospital where their mother died about an hour ago. I don't know what to think, and I guess they don't know how to handle it either."*

Can you imagine what I felt at that moment? Suddenly I *SAW* things differently . . . and because I *saw* things differently, I *thought* differently, I *felt* differently, I *behaved* differently. My irritation vanished. I didn't have to worry about controlling my attitude or my behavior. My *HEART* was filled with the man's pain. Feelings of *sympathy* and *compassion* flowed freely.

"Oh, I'm so sorry! *Can you tell me about it? What can I do to help?"* Everything changed in an instant!

In that instant, the author's perspective changed and he saw through the ***eyes of his Heart***. He was able to look with the compassionate "*Heart of a Caregiver*" ... to look beyond the behavior to the *NEEDS* of those who were hurting ... to look on them with ***Empathy*** and treat them with an extra measure of *Kindness*, *Mercy* and *Grace*.

"There are two parts to Empathy:
Skill - tip of the iceberg ...
Attitude - mass of the iceberg."

—Author Unknown

"Empathy opens the eyes of your HEART to see beyond the words and behavior of the person on the outside . . . to the feelings and intents of the person on the inside."

— Author Unknown

ONE TOUGH COWBOY

*from **Love Your Patients***
by Scott Louis Diering, M.D.

When I practiced in western Nebraska, I treated a lot of cowboys and rodeo riders. I had one patient with an obvious shoulder dislocation. He was sweating, gripping the stretcher, and almost crying. I said, *"I think you need some pain medications before X-rays."*

He replied through gritted teeth, gasping, *"No doc, it's okay, it don't hurt too much."*

Here was a critical choice-point. Do I believe his **words** (*"No doc, it's okay . . ."*) or his **actions and expressions** (sweating, holding on to the stretcher, etc.) which said he was in a lot of pain?

I chose to read the obvious clues he was giving me. I explained to him, *"This type of injury usually hurts a lot. Even though you are not hurting too badly, **I** would feel better if I could give you some pain medicine."* He agreed to an IV, and accepted the morphine.

"OK, doc," he winced, *"but just for you."* We both felt a lot better.

I chose to **Empathize** with this patient. I could have accepted his verbal statement, documented his refusal of pain medication, and sent him to X-ray. However, this would not have been good care. *I empathized.*

I read his non-verbal cues and acted on those cues by explaining what would make *me* feel better. I never asked my patient to admit he was in pain, nor did I explain to him he did not need to appear macho in an ER. I told him how *I* felt, and I asked him if he would make *me* feel better.

Although his pain was a key part of my empathy, I also empathized with his need to be tough and refuse pain medications. I could relate to his pain . . . I could almost feel his pain by his look and posture. At the same time, I could sense his need to be tough, and his desire to not cry and not beg for relief.

I would never have given him pain medications if he continued to refuse them: It's his right to refuse. But I understood him, and he understood me, and together we agreed on a management course that benefited us both.

"One of the most valuable things we can do to **HEAL** one another is **LISTEN** to each other's stories."

— Rebecca Falls

Some people cope with their pain and frustration by complaining to anyone who will listen . . .

They don't necessarily expect the pain and problems to go away, but they do hope for and need an empathetic listener . . . someone who will LISTEN and understand . . .
Empathy works like magic!

TWO MAGIC WORDS
"I'M SORRY"

by Paula J. Fox

When patients are upset or hurt . . . You're there to lend a hand
And it helps for them to know
how much you *HEAR* and *understand*.

When you say to them . . .*"I'm sorry"* . . . it shows **Empathy** and *Care*
It expresses that you're on their side . . .
you know the pain they bear.

These words don't say you're guilty . . . There is nothing you did wrong
They just show how much you *Empathize*
with what is going on.

"I'm sorry you are hurting." . . . *"I'm so sorry you're in pain."*
"I'm sorry that you have to
do this over once again."

"I'm sorry that you feel this way." . . . *"I'm sorry it's not fair."*
"I'm sorry that you had to wait." . . .
"I'm sorry no one's there."

"I'm sorry this has happened" . . . *"I'm sorry* you're so sad."
"I know this must be hard for you . . .
I'm sorry it's so bad."

These words convey your *Caring Heart* and help to ease the stress
They can calm an angry soul
and bring a sense of peace and rest

Two magic words with universal power and appeal
When they're spoken from the *Heart* . . .
they can help the spirit *HEAL*.

"Perhaps True Healing has more to do
with LISTENING and unconditional LOVE
than with trying to fix people."

-- GERALD JAMPOLSKY, M.D.

"Empathy enables
us to go inside the
HEART of another
to visit for a while."

— Paula J. Fox

CONNECTING HEART TO HEART

by Hannah Fox, RN, BSN

He was a very frail man, small in stature, old in years and very ill, but Mr. P had a significant influence on my career as a *Nurse*. I met him while I was still in nursing school, working as an extern on a renal and oncology floor.

When I first started, I really wanted to be *efficient*! I had my *checklist* of things to get done . . . blood draws, vitals, baths, and getting people up to walk. Mr. P changed my whole perspective on *Nursing care*. He helped me to see the person inside the body and to truly *CARE* for my patients.

I met this gentleman when I came into his room one day to help him out of bed and into a chair to sit up for his allotted time. We worked together very slowly, step by step, as I guided him along. When he was finally in the chair, I propped him up with pillows under his arms and legs and made sure the pillows were adjusted just right under his head and behind his back for added support and cushion.

Since I had just finished my first year of nursing school, I had learned all the ways you can position a patient in a bed or chair, especially with the aid of pillows. It was exciting for me to take this "task" of getting Mr. P into a chair as an opportunity to put to use what I had just learned in school.

When we were finished he looked up at me with tears in his eyes, and said, **"No one has ever taken the time** *to get me so comfortable sitting in this chair."*

Not knowing how to respond, I said, *"Oh, well, I'm just doing my job."*

Mr. P replied, *"No, you spent the time to get me in the chair, AND get me comfortable, and* **that means you CARE** *and you're good at what you do."* I leaned over and gave him a hug, because I didn't know what else to say in that moment.

The next day, I was eager to go visit Mr. P because he had really made an impression on me, and I loved feeling that "bond" between us. When I came in, he gave me a great big smile, and we began the process of getting him up in the chair again. When we were done, he told me a story of a beautiful German girl he met when he was stationed in Germany during WWII. He explained that I reminded him of her and then asked if he could sing me a German love song that he had learned to sing for her.

As he sang, I was deeply moved. I remember thinking, *"This is why I want to be a Nurse . . . for this feeling of **connecting with a complete stranger**, for the feeling of knowing you gave them a bright spot in their day, even if they are struggling."* Another nurse came in to hear the song as well and when we left Mr. P's room she told me that he had been a "grumpy old man" before I came.

I can still remember the day I came in and met his family who were all there to say goodbye. He passed away quietly and once again, I got him cleaned up and comfortable. It was the first time I had to do post-mortem care, but I was honored to do so. He touched my life and influenced how I practice as a *Nurse* to this day.

Mr. P taught me that it's *NOT* just about *"getting it done."* It's about *"**connecting heart to heart** "* with my patients . . . going the extra mile, making them comfortable even if it takes a little more time, and really *CARING* for them as individuals.

"Live your life from your Heart.

Share from your Heart.

And your story will Touch and

HEAL people's souls."

— Melody Beattie

Comfort

. . . is the precious **Healing Presence** within the *HEART of a Caregiver* . . . designed to help relieve suffering and expressed through compassionate loving *CARE.*

It can be seen in the way you touch the hearts of your patients with a *kind sensitive manner* and in the way you comfort their bodies and souls with a *tender physical touch.* Even when your patients' pain is manifested in rude behavior, you offer empathy and understanding from a *Caregiver's Heart.*

Comfort goes beyond the physical realm . . . for as one who *CARES,* you minister to the emotional needs of your patients as well. Your *Caring HEART* is a safe haven for hurting people, a place where they can bring their broken hearts as well as their broken bodies.

Sometimes you can relieve the pain, and sometimes you can just ease their suffering and make them a little more comfortable . . . but you always make a difference with a *HEART* that *CARES.*

"We may not cure their cancer, or bring their baby back to life, or reverse their Alzheimer's. However, we can touch them, COMFORT them, and make a difference. With just a little love, we can make their suffering more tolerable."

— Scott Louis Diering, M.D.

WHEN I CANNOT CURE, I CAN STILL CARE

Meg D., RN, BSN -- Columbus, Ohio

"Are you going to be assigned to Mrs. S today?" asked the nurse.

When I answered "yes," she said in a whisper, *"Before you go in there, there is something you should know. About five seconds ago, the doctor informed her that she has a massive malignancy in her left breast. Likely, it's terminal. The poor woman is an absolute wreck. I've never seen anyone shaking so badly. She keeps saying she doesn't know what to do. Perhaps you can get through to her."*

Mrs. S was crying quietly when I walked in. My first impulse was to cry, too, or to say something profound, something that would "make it all better." Instead, I took her hand, looked her in the face, and said softly, *"I'm Meg. I'm going to stay with you until 3 this afternoon. Your night nurse told me what the doctors just told you. I want you to know that it's OK to cry as much as you want."*

"Cure sometimes, treat often, comfort always."

— Hippocrates

It was as if I'd given her the "permission" she needed. Mrs. S began sobbing as I finished speaking, clutching my hand and murmuring the jumbled words that come when pain is just too deep for expression. I sat next to her on the bed as she cried, just holding her hand.

I learned many things from Mrs. S that day. I learned how life is precious even to the elderly, and how even when staring in the face of death, one struggles to eek out just one little bit more of the life that is left.

When I discovered the source of the cancer, a black, crusted crater in Mrs. S's left breast that easily accommodated my entire fist, I learned about the crazy dance of denial, the unwillingness to surrender this experience called life.

Most importantly I learned . . . *Even* **when I cannot cure, I can still CARE**. *Nursing care doesn't always have to involve bedpans or IV pumps or high tech machinery . . . but it must always, always, ALWAYS involve the HEART.*

"I've slowly learned that there is invariably
at least one thing one can do:
Stay there . . . Sit and listen as someone cries.
Stroke their arm. Hold their hand.
Acknowledge your sorrow at their suffering . . .
Don't walk away."

—ELISABETH OCHS, RN

"The Most Precious Gift we can offer others is our Presence. Touching deeply is an important practice. We touch with our hands, our eyes, our ears and also with our mindfulness."

— Thich Nhat Hanh

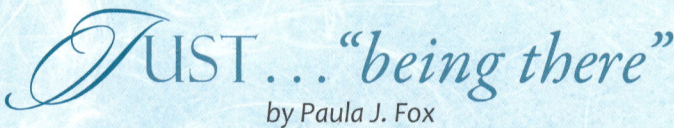

JUST..."being there"

by Paula J. Fox

Sometimes there is nothing we can say or do
to make those who are hurting feel better.
And we'd rather walk away than watch them suffer,
so we don't have to experience their pain.

The *Heart of a Caregiver*, however, never walks away,
but makes a *choice* to help, even if it means
just ***"being there"*** to offer emotional support . . .
partnering with them through their pain.

I heard a story about a young American woman
who experienced the simplicity and power
of this special kind of *Comfort*
while working with Mother Teresa in Calcutta.

The young woman's job was to rub oil on the women
who came to the ashram, sick and hurting in body and spirit.
One day an older Indian woman was brought in
after her husband threw hot wax over most of her body.

This woman was in great pain, near death,
and could not tolerate anyone touching her at all.
The younger woman knew she certainly
couldn't help her by rubbing oil on her body.

She also knew she couldn't comfort her with words
because they each spoke a different language.
All she had to offer was her presence . . . just *"being there"*
with her so she would not have to suffer alone.

So she sat down beside her, giving her full attention,
looking into her eyes with deep compassion and care.
They sat in silence together without saying a word,
but with a common bond of understanding.

Suddenly the Indian woman reached up and
took the young woman's face in her blistered hands,
kissing her in a spontaneous gesture of gratitude.
A few hours later she died peacefully.

The young woman's *PRESENCE* with her during her final hours
made all the difference!

"He who becomes a brother to the bruised, a doctor to the despairing, and a

COMFORTER

to the crushed may not actually say much . . . . What he has to offer is often beyond the power of speech to convey. But the weary sense it, and it is the balm of Gilead to their souls."

— Vance Havner

THE COMFORT OF A TOUCH

by Paula J. Fox

Healthcare is very special. In no other job are you given instant intimacy with another person and allowed to touch them in such a tender personal way. Your touch can provide healing and comfort to those who are sick, those who are hurting, and those who have experienced loss and sorrow.

> *"There are those whose hands have sunbeams in them*
> *so that their grasp warms my heart."*
>
> —*Helen Keller*

I was recently reminded that it is not only those who are in obvious distress that need a *Caring* tender touch. We all need to be touched once in a while . . . to connect with another human being in a warm, loving way.

As I was walking out of church one morning, I happened to see a close friend I had known for years, and we hugged each other warmly. I greeted another friend who was with her as well, but we did not embrace, and the three of us visited for a few minutes before moving on.

Afterwards, I had a slightly uneasy feeling as I reflected on my brief encounter with these two dear ladies, both of whom have lost their husbands, both of whom live alone. These words from a poem that I had recently read came back to haunt me ...

"How long has it been since someone touched me?
Twenty years?... Twenty years I've been a widow.
Respected ... Smiled at ... But NEVER touched.
Never held so close that loneliness was blotted out."

— from "Minnie Remembers" by Donna Swanson

My heart suddenly ached for the friend I had not *touched* that morning, and I promised myself that I would give her a hug the very next time I saw her. What a poignant reminder that we need to be more sensitive to others and their need to be tenderly touched, especially those who live alone!

As I thought about my friends, I also vowed that from that moment on, I would be more generous with my hugs, and I would try to give more caring touches . . . a two-handed greeting, a gentle arm around the shoulder, or just softly taking a hand to hold.

Everyone needs to be touched . . . to feel loved and affirmed. It is a well-documented fact that babies who are held thrive much better than those who are not. But the truth is that we never outgrow our need to be touched in a nurturing, tender way. This is especially true for those who are hurting, those who are lonely, and those who feel unloved and useless.

What a *COMFORT* and *blessing* it is when a *Caregiver* provides that very special ***Tender Touch*** from the ***HEART!***

"All of us benefit from touch.
You can be quite isolated without
touch and very lonely ...
There's something about having
another human being

Caring and Touching you that
makes you feel good inside."

— Evelyn Youngberg, D.O.N.

Dr. Allan Sawyer is one of the kindest, most caring doctors you will ever meet, loved by patients and nurses alike. His insight into good nursing CARE is based on years of experience working with nurses in many states across the United States, as well as in Kenya and Papua, New Guinea. As he reflects on the qualities that make a nurse so special, he paints for us a picture of the true HEART of a Caregiver.

"One person **CARING** about another represents life's greatest value."

— Jim Rohn

A DOCTOR REFLECTS ON NURSES

by Allan T. Sawyer, M.D.

After a quarter century of working with *Nurses*... those who possess these qualities are the ones who have *touched my HEART* the most:

❯ the *Nurses* who *SEE* the **person** *BEHIND* the smell, the cancer and the disease and genuinely seek to bring *healing* and *comfort* to each patient;

❯ the *Nurses* who not only **weep compassionately** for a patient while holding their hand, but then go outside the room and continue to weep compassionately for what they have just seen and experienced;

❯ the *Nurses* who have **prayed** for the patients whom they are going to **serve** that day, even before they have met them;

❯ the *Nurses* who **rejoice** with patients who are rejoicing;

... who **cry** with those who are crying;

... who **hurt** with those who are hurting;

... who **laugh** with those who are laughing;

... who **lend courage** to those who are fearful;

... who **educate** those who need to be taught;

... who **selflessly serve** those who need to be served.

"Do all the good you can.
By all the means you can.
In all the ways you can.
In all the places you can.
At all the times you can.
To all the people you can.
As long as ever you can."

—John Wesley

Generosity

. . . is the **Selfless Giving** that flows from the *HEART of a Caregiver*, motivated by genuine love and concern for others.

"You give but little when you give of your possessions.
*It is when you **give of yourself** that you truly give."*
—*Kahlil Gibran*

The needs of a patient are ongoing, and like the "Energizer Bunny," your generous *Caring HEART* just keeps **giving and giving** . . . often giving more of yourself than is required and certainly sometimes more than is deserved.

Your generosity can be defined in terms of *Mercy* and *Grace*. It is common knowledge that *"hurt people **hurt** people"* . . . but the *Caring HEART* is able to look beyond the behavior of the patient to a hurting heart.

You extend *Mercy* by forgiving any unkindness and offer *Grace* by giving **generous loving CARE** even to the most difficult patient.

"Today, see if you can stretch your

HEART

and expand your love so that it touches not
only those to whom you can give it easily,
but also those who need it so much."

— Daphne Rose Kingma

 ANGELS OF MERCY

by Paula J. Fox

As she told me her story I saw in her eyes . . .
she was sorry that it was all true.
The cancer had caused her to act out in ways
that she normally never would do.

One final treatment was all she had left . . .
and the battle was almost won.
Then the doctor informed her that more was required
. . . and she wasn't nearly done.

That was the moment she suddenly snapped. . .
and she just couldn't face more pain.
She broke down completely and screamed at them all,
"I'm NOT coming back again!!!"

She continued to rant and rave at the *Nurses*,
"I HATE you! You TORTURE me so!"
As she humbly recounted this story, she said . . .
"It wasn't their fault, you know."

What amazed her the most was the *Nurses'* response . . .
to her ugly and hateful display.
Their kind and gentle compassionate hearts
gave the gift of *Forgiveness* that day.

No wonder they're often called ***ANGELS OF MERCY*** . . .
they see people at their worst.
But shining their light in the midst of the darkness,
they offer them *Kindness* first.

They know it's the fear and pain that is speaking . . .
so they try not to judge or condemn.
Instead of giving back what they deserve
they give *Mercy* and *Grace* to them.

ANGELS . . . are God's special messengers . . .
as they minister here on earth.
And *Nurses,* like *Angels* . . . bring *Hope* to their patients,
reaffirming their value and worth.

Forgiving the hurts and the awful behavior . . .
and forgetting the words so unfair,
MERCY . . . can calm and soothe the spirit
with compassionate *Comfort* and *Care.*

It's a quality found in the *Heart of a Nurse* . . .
perhaps the most beautiful part.
When an *ANGEL of MERCY* touches the soul
. . . it's divinely inspired *ART!*

The "ART" of Nursing...

"A person who works
with his hands is a laborer.

A person who works with his hands
and his brain is a craftsman.

But the person who works
with his hands and his brain and his HEART
is an ARTIST."

— Louis Nizer

"When LOVE and SKILL work together, expect a Masterpiece."

— John Ruskin

TAKING PART IN MIRACLES

by Julia Cho

Often, you wake in the morning when it's still dark
and dress quietly so you don't wake anyone.
You steal away to work through streets without cars,
without people.
You know the way well.

The hospital is like a city;
it has its own generator, its own rhythms, its own customs.
You know it like your own house.
You come here day after night after day
and see people in the moments when their lives change.

You see women turned into mothers
and babies into sons and daughters.
You see men turned into fathers
and couples turned into families.
Sometimes it's easy to forget that you are witness to such
MIRACLES.

Most of the time your feet hurt
or you're a little out of shape
or you forget to eat
or any number of a thousand things
that all need your attention right now, yesterday.

But it will all have to wait because right now
the call button is going off,
or the phone is ringing, or there is someone
who is hungry or cold or afraid of pain
and you are *the one who responds.*

It would be impossible to gather together in one place,
all the people whose lives you have touched.
So we say the words now that all of them . . .
all these women, mothers, babies, sons, daughters, men,
fathers, couples, and families would say if they could.

THANK YOU . . . Thank you for being
the one who responds. Thank you for being
the one who cares for those who are overwhelmed
and those who can't care for themselves. There are
other jobs that are far easier and demand far less.

Sleepless days and nights you come here,
ready to give of yourself, and then, even when you're spent,
even when there's nothing left, you give just a little bit more.
No one who does not do your work
could ever understand how difficult it is.

And we don't know how you do it.
How you comfort others even when you yourself need comfort.
How you tend to others even when you yourself are tired.
You may be present at miracles
but the *MIRACLE* is also, quite simply . . . *YOU!*

"If someone listens, or stretches
out a hand, or whispers a kind word
of encouragement, or attempts
to understand a lonely person . . .

EXTRAORDINARY

things begin to happen."

— Loretta Girzartis

"The effect of
ONE
good-hearted person is
INCALCULABLE."

— Oscar Arias

ALWAYS A NURSE

by Noelle Trinder, RN, BSN, PCCN, CNRN

I do not stop being a *Nurse* at 5:00 p.m.

I am ALWAYS a Nurse.

My neighbor calls late one night.
She cries while we pray together about her upcoming surgery.

I am ALWAYS a Nurse.

An elderly woman is lost in the grocery store.
I stop, offer my arm, and help her find her concerned son.

I am ALWAYS a Nurse.

A toddler stumbles in the parking lot.
Crocodile tears flood her eyes. I give a band-aid and a loving hug.

I am ALWAYS a Nurse.

My family members ask advice about
medications and odd-looking moles.

I am ALWAYS a Nurse.

It's show-and-tell at preschool, and my
daughter brings Mommy because, *"She helps people."*

I am ALWAYS a Nurse.

When I stop being a *Nurse*, I stop being me.

I am ALWAYS a Nurse.

"Caregivers don't
always have the time …
but they have the HEART,
so they make the time."

— Author Unknown

Kindness

. . . is the **Loving Behavior** that is characteristic of the *HEART of a Caregiver* . . . adding value to others through words, actions and attitudes.

It is the special tenderness that is seen in the little things you do. Your understanding look, your soft gentle touch, your attentive way of listening, and every kind gesture or expression of your *Caring HEART* affirms others and shows them that you really *CARE*.

Kindness is the beautiful quality that sets you apart in your field as one who possesses the true *Caregiver's Heart*. You *choose* to be *KIND*. You are deliberately tuned in to your patients, and always respond with sensitivity to the unique needs of each individual.

When you treat your patients with dignity and respect, regardless of who they are or how they act, you make them feel special and lift their spirits. It is one of the most endearing qualities and certainly the most *visible* attribute of the *Heart* that **CARES**.

"**KINDNESS** is more than deeds.
It is an attitude, an expression, a look, a touch.
It is anything that lifts another person."

— C. Neil Strait

ALL IN A DAY'S WORK

by Naomi Rhode

Emergency-room personnel transported him to the cardiac floor. Long hair, unshaven, dirty, dangerously obese and a black motorcycle jacket tossed on the bottom shelf of the stretcher—an outsider to this sterile world of shining terrazzo floors, efficient uniformed professionals and strict infection-control procedures. Definitely an untouchable!

The nurses at the station looked wide-eyed as this mound of humanity was wheeled by—each glancing nervously at my friend Bonnie, the head nurse. *"Let this one not be mine to admit, bathe, and tend to...."* was the pleading, unspoken message from their inner concern.

One of the true marks of a leader, a consummate professional, is to do the unthinkable. To touch the untouchable. To tackle the impossible. Yes, it was Bonnie who said, *"I want this patient myself."* Highly unusual for a head nurse—unconventional—but "the stuff" out of which human spirits thrive, heal and soar.

As she donned her latex gloves and proceeded to bathe this huge, filthy man, her heart almost broke. *Where was his family? Who was his mother? What was he like as a little boy?*

She hummed quietly as she worked to ease the fear and embarrassment she knew he must have been feeling. And then on a whim she said, *"We don't have time for back rubs much in hospitals these days, but I bet one would really feel good. And, it would help you relax your muscles and start to heal. That is what this place is all about—a place to heal."*

All in a day's work. ***Touching the untouchable.***

"Even the
smallest act of kindness says...
'I CARE'...
says 'You matter'...
says 'I thought of you.'"

— Sir Arthur Helps

His thick, scaly, ruddy skin told a story of an abusive lifestyle. Probably lots of addictive behavior to food, alcohol and drugs. As Bonnie rubbed the taut muscles, she hummed and prayed. Prayed for the soul of a little boy grown up, rejected by life's rudeness and striving for acceptance in a hard, hostile world.

The finale—warmed lotion and baby powder. Almost laughable—such a contrast on this huge, rugged surface. As he rolled over onto his back, tears rolled down his cheek. With amazingly beautiful brown eyes, he smiled and said in a quivering voice, *"No one has touched me for years."* His chin trembled. *"Thank you. I am healing."*

In a day when we have increasing concern about the appropriateness of touch, Bonnie taught this hurting world to still dare to touch the untouchable through eye contact, a warm handshake, a concerned voice—or the physical reassurance of warmed lotion and baby powder.

"Just because an animal is large,
it doesn't mean he doesn't want

KINDNESS.

However big Tigger seems to be,
remember that he wants as
much kindness as Roo."

— Winnie The Pooh

"We are here to change the world with small acts of thoughtfulness done daily rather than with one great breakthrough."

— Rabbi Harold Kushner

BECAUSE THEY CARE

by Paula J. Fox

They often must work without enough staff.
There are so many things to do.
Besides *CARING* for all of your physical needs ...
they have charting and records too.

It's not that they don't have compassionate hearts.
They chose nursing because they *CARE*.
But sometimes with all of the constant demands ...
it's all they can do to be there.

So give them a break when response time seems slow.
They're busier than you may think.
Sometimes it's hard to even find time ...
for a bathroom break or a drink!

"Bound by paperwork,
short on hands, sleep, and energy . . .
nurses are rarely short on

CARING."

—Sharon Hudacek, *A Daybook for Nurses*

NIGHTINGALE'S LAMP

by Noelle Trinder, RN, BSN, PCCN, CNRN

I wonder what Florence Nightingale would think of her *Nurses* now. She was the original pioneer in the *Art of Nursing,* a true hero of her time, dedicated to *Serving* others and *Caring* for the sick and injured. She would check on her patients (soldiers of the Crimean War) at night by carrying a lamp and became known as ***"The Lady with the LAMP."***

Sometimes I get caught up in the *technical* aspect of *Nursing,* as I am sure, *Nurses,* you can relate . . . answering calls from doctors, completing computer charting on time, looking at the patient's vital signs, completing blood sugar checks, reading the heart monitors, passing medications, starting cardiac drips to regulate heart rate, etc., etc. Whew!

In those crazy times, I ask you to stop and take a minute to remember Florence Nightingale. I know some of the patients do.

"So, Nightingale, where is your LAMP?" asked John, a 78-year-old patient I was caring for with end-stage lung cancer. He was labored

in his breathing, and I could hear the whistle noise his lungs were making as he wheezed in and out with every breath.

I adjusted his IV drip, concentrating to make sure the dosing was correct. I hit the "start" button on the vital signs machine and watched it tighten on his arm. The blood pressure read low as did his oxygen level. I pushed the call bell . . . *"Susan, I need a STAT breathing treatment to room eight."*

"John, I need to call the doctor for further orders. Your vital signs are reading low, and he needs to be aware. I will be right back," I said and started to pull the curtain to exit the room.

"Wait, Nurse, where is your LAMP?" he asked again. I was concerned about his status and needed to call the doctor. But, in this moment, I remembered Florence Nightingale and her commitment to *Serving* and *Caring*.

"Ok," I moved back into the room, *"let me call the doctor from your phone then, and I'll answer your question."* I sat down on the bed next

to John, held his hand, and dialed the doctor's number. Country music played as I held for the doctor's answering service.

"I don't have a lamp. I guess they don't use those anymore, John. I think they were replaced in the '80s with pen lights." We both laughed, and then he said, *"Honestly . . . **just stay a minute. I'm scared.**"*

"I will stay, and I am here for you, deep breaths, John." I continued to hold his hand until I reached the doctor by phone.

It was five minutes, and the most refreshing five minutes I had all day. It brought my work back into focus. *Under all the IVs, blood pressure cuffs and oxygen tubing is a PERSON . . . my patient. I am his Nurse, his lifeline, his advocate, and his family.*

People in the community trust a *Nurse*. I am honored by that trust and am committed to *serving* those I come in contact with. **Nursing is not only a profession . . . It's a way of life.** It's in everything we do, and everywhere we go. And Florence Nightingale is right there next to us, reminding us to focus and bring our *"LAMP"* in the fast-paced nursing world of today.

"There are persons so radiant, so genial, so KIND, so pleasure-bearing, that you instinctively feel in their presence that they do you good; whose coming into a room is like bringing a LAMP there."

— Henry Ward Beecher

"You're here to be
LIGHT...Shine!
Be generous with
your lives."

from *The Message* by Eugene H. Peterson

Sometimes the kindest thing we can do for others is to remind them that they still have value and they can be a benefit to others. I wrote this poem as a reminder that everyone has something to give, even if it's only a smile, a bit of wisdom, or a positive example of good character.

NEVER TOO OLD

by Paula J. Fox

He longs to regain some control of his life . . .
It's been lost along the way. His health is poor.
He can no longer drive, dependent on others each day.

It's hard to accept the inevitable . . . Growing old
isn't easy to do. It takes inner strength and
courage at times . . . just to make it through.

The days can be long and terribly lonely . . . Sometimes
they're filled with pain. But the thing that is always
the hardest to bear . . . is to never feel useful again.

Everyone needs a purpose in life . . . something
to live for each day . . . A way to contribute
to others in need . . . and never just fade away.

The Bible reminds us we're **never too old** . . . to be
VALUED and useful to God. We don't have to be strong
in a physical way. . . That kind of thinking is flawed.

There are lots of important things still to give . . .
like *joy* and *wisdom* and *grace* . . . encouraging others,
inspiring faith . . . and putting a smile on each face.

It's the time to focus on finishing well . . . with character
to go the distance. The victories won with
inner strength . . . give life its real ***Significance.***

*"The greatest good you can do for another is not just
to share your riches, but to reveal to him his own."*
— BENJAMIN DISRAELI

Encouragement

. . . is the life-giving **Source of Power** in the *HEART of a Caregiver* . . . delivering *Light* in the darkness to those who are weary and hurting.

As you walk into each room, you bring comfort and *Hope* with the possibility of relief from pain and anxiety. You quiet troubled minds as you take time to answer questions and provide much needed information.

You inspire the hearts of your patients as you cheer them on and give them a vision of their own strength and courage. You can empower them with your positive attitude and words of affirmation, celebrating with them every small victory and success.

A happy heart is good medicine and you can brighten the day for each person you meet with a smile, a compliment, or a word of encouragement from a *Heart* that **CARES**.

"Believe that there's a
LIGHT
at the end of the tunnel.
Believe that
YOU
might be that light for
someone else."

— Kobi Yamada

PAINTERS OF LIGHT

by Paula J. Fox

Everyone knows that *Nurses* are skilled . . .
in the science and technical arts
But they're equally gifted in creative ways
that require more sensitive hearts

These talented artists are ***"Painters of Light"*** . . .
transforming the darkest places
With the radiant glow of compassionate *CARE*
they bring smiles to saddened faces

They are masters of this luminous craft . . .
using ***Light*** to brighten each day
erasing the shadows of worry and fear
to help make the pain go away

All living things need ***Light*** to survive . . .
to be physically healthy and strong
And the powerful ***Light*** of positive thoughts
gives strength when the nights are long

Nurses are called to carry the ***Light*** . . .
to those who are in despair
filled with a passion for helping others
from the depths of their souls . . . they *CARE!*

With a cheerful manner and a warm disposition . . .
they relieve anxiety
When they walk in a room, they can *"turn on the **Lights**"*
of hope and tranquility

With each tender stroke, the ***Light*** will emerge . . .
so the patient begins to see
It takes genius . . . and art . . . and inspiration
Nurses encompass all three

They can brighten a day with small acts of kindness . . .
adding highlights and moments of *joy*
Their **Light** can *EMPOWER* and energize
. . . or calm a scared little boy

Light can make us feel *safe* and *secure* . . .
(In the dark, things always look black)
Nurses are always there to protect you
like heroes who cover your back

This world would be a much darker place . . .
without them to shine so bright
Touching lives with their own special radiance,
Nurses are . . . ***Painters of Light***

"A kind heart is like a candle that can be used to light dozens
of others without losing any of its own flame."

— Steve Deger

"There is a candle in every soul,
some brightly burning . . .
some dark and cold.

Carry your candle. Run to the darkness.
Seek out the hopeless,
confused and torn.

Hold out your candle for all to see it.
Take your candle . . .
go LIGHT your world!"

— Excerpt from *Go Light Your World*
by Kathy Troccoli

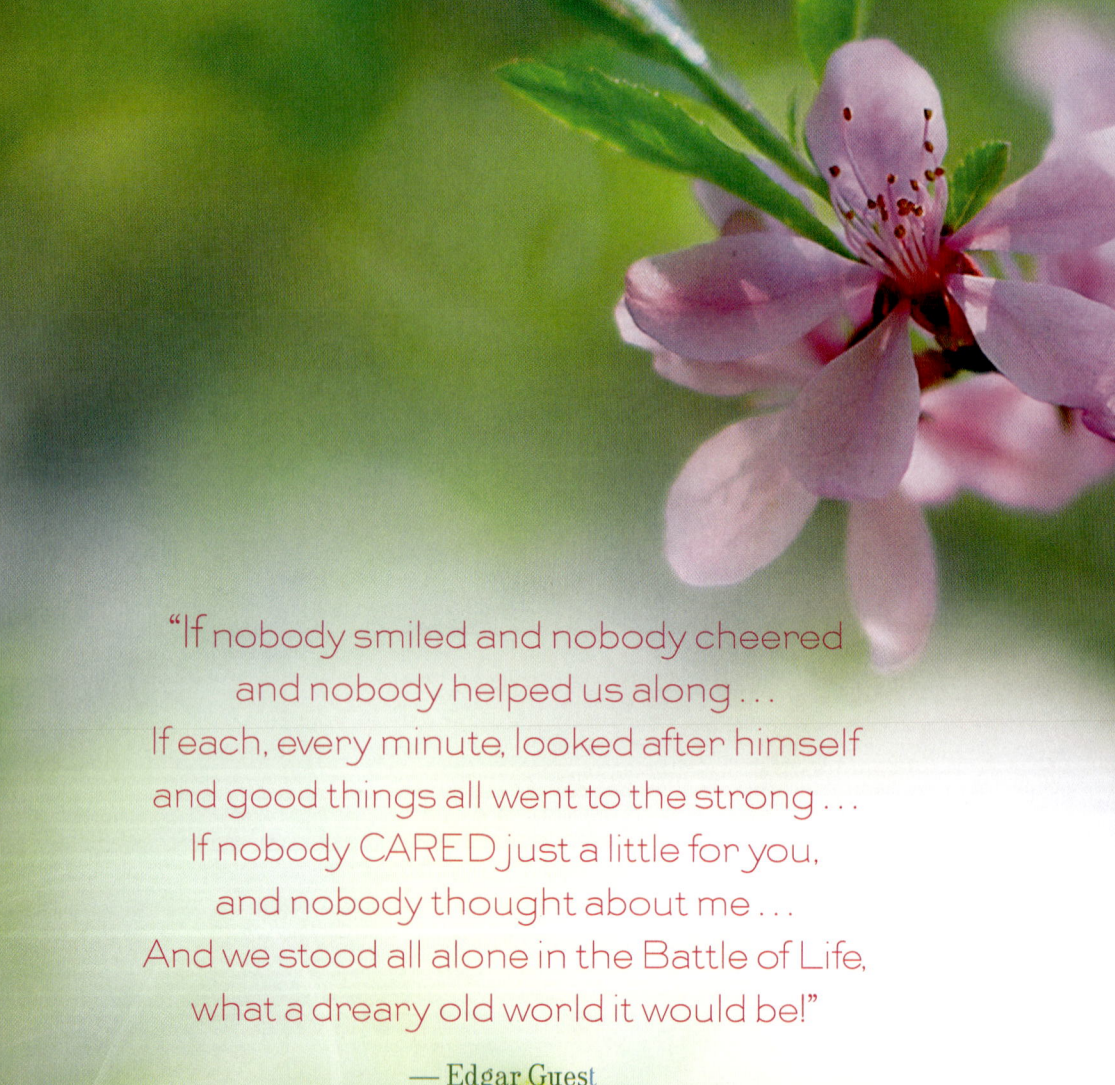

"If nobody smiled and nobody cheered
and nobody helped us along . . .
If each, every minute, looked after himself
and good things all went to the strong . . .
If nobody CARED just a little for you,
and nobody thought about me . . .
And we stood all alone in the Battle of Life,
what a dreary old world it would be!"

— Edgar Guest

CAREGIVER'S HANDBOOK
By Beverly Haley

I heard the sounds of car doors opening and shutting and nine-year-old Ellen's eager hop-skippity. In the flick of an eyelash she stood at the door, arms stretched wide. *"Grandma, I've been missing you!"* The radiance of that smile made me forget the punishing weight of relentless July heat.

Her arms locked around my waist, her head pressed against my chest. I looked down.

"New shoes?"

She nodded. *"Fast ones,"* she said, then announced, *"I came to give Grandpa a big hug."*

Red flags whipped from my *Caregiver's* antennae. For the bezillionth time in the past three years, my frustration level shot off the chart. I needed a *Caregiving* how-to book where I could run my finger down the table of contents, point to a key word, flip to that page, and read the answer. Should I let her see him?

I drew Ellen closer and gazed over her to meet my son's eyes. She'd seen her grandpa two days ago, but.... *"He's much worse,"* I mouthed. *"Seeing him might frighten her."*

My son's gaze held steady. *"She'll be all right, Mom. She needs to hug him."* I felt compelled to protect her. Would she store up nightmare images that frightened away memories of his healthy years?

And I felt just as compelled to protect my husband. Yesterday's words from our hospice nurse still echoed sharply inside me. *"He needs to relax and let go,"* she'd advised. *"Distractions now will disrupt the dying process."* How could I take responsibility for even a single minute's extra suffering? Yet how could I deny either of them a last hug? I teetered on the edge of denial and consent. Where *was* that **Caregiver's Handbook**?

My son's arm circled my shoulders. *"She'll be okay, Mom, I know."*

My emotional teetering steadied. I nodded at Ellen, whose face glowed with expectation. *"He's sleeping,"* I said, *"but he'll wake when he knows you're there."*

Tip-toeing into the bedroom, she gazed at the still, slight form beneath the covers. In seconds she was on the bed beside him, arms gentle around his neck. He turned to her with a sun-and-stars smile that matched hers. *"Hello, Ellen. How's my buddy?"*

"I love you, Papa," she said.

"I love you, too."

She snuggled beside him, stroking his face. *"I have new sneakers."*

"They'll help you run faster," he said. His eyelids grew heavy.

My son signaled Ellen and with a farewell pat on Grandpa's shoulder, she climbed down.

"Did I help him feel better, Grandma?"

"Yes, you did. Much better." I watched as he rolled again to the place where his body rested more at ease. Leaving him, the three of us moved to the cool shade of the deck for ice cream bars.

"I wish he could get well," Ellen said. *"But I'm glad I made him smile."*

"Yes, and he gave you the best smile ever."

Last week she'd asked when he would get better. I'd tried to explain that he couldn't get well, that his body had used up all its strength. The cancer, I told her, was taking his body, but it could never take away who he really is—his sparkling smile, the light in his eyes, his love for her.

Looking back on the countless teams of *Caregivers*—the teams shifting and changing with each new twist and turn, every team giving their all to his care—I saw that Ellen herself had been a constant. For the entire three years of his illness, her steel thread of *Caregiving* never wavered. She brought a kind of *Caregiving* no one else could offer, partly out of the innocence of childhood.

How do you tell a child about dying? How do you tell her that soon Grandpa won't be with us?

How I yearned for that *Caregiver's* book. As she ate her ice cream bar she said, *"I'll miss him, Grandma. It makes me sad."* After a moment her brown eyes grew round. *"Will he be an angel soon?"*

"Yes, he'll be an angel watching over us even when we can't see him. And he'll stay in our hearts always."

My son knew his little girl. She had needed to see her Grandpa one more time. I thought about how as a teenager I'd felt hurt and left out when my parents kept me from seeing my dying grandmother. Now I'd nearly repeated history, trying to protect my own granddaughter.

Did her visit disrupt his dying process? Maybe. But her farewell touch gave a loving grandfather a last moment's earthly treasure. He, in turn, gave the gift of that moment back to her, to our son, and to me.

Ellen didn't need a **Caregiver's Handboo**k. She opened her *HEART* and followed it.

"There is not enough darkness in all the world to put out the LIGHT of even the smallest candle."

— Robert Alden

"I have seldom seen anything **LIGHT UP THE FACES** of elderly residents in care facilities more quickly than a cat or dog or a young child . In either case, people sitting slumped in wheelchairs and apparently sleeping, perk up, smile and reach out their hands."

— Dawn Nelson

UNCONDITIONAL LOVE

by Paula J. Fox

An elderly man in a nursing home bed
was grumpy and not at all kind
He yelled at the nurses and doctors alike
and gave them a piece of his mind

He was known to make life pretty miserable
for everyone charged with his care
His anger and sadness spilled over on others . . .
affecting whoever was there

No visitors came to his bedside to cheer him
It seemed no one loved him at all
Then one day his heart found a reason to *smile*
when a four-legged "friend" came to call

This sweet old dog was wagging her tail
as if to say, *"Hi there, my friend!"*
Walking over to lay her head on his bed,
she gently nuzzled his hand

You could soon see the tears well up in his eyes
as he tenderly patted her head
In that moment in time he completely forgot
that he felt so trapped in his bed

The **comfort** of such unconditional *LOVE*
and the touch of her soft silky fur
was just the prescription he needed to heal . . .
a *"therapy dog"* . . . just like her

What a blessing we now allow ***"angels with paws"***
to visit each nursing home floor.
Bringing *JOY* to so many like this lonely soul
the minute she walks through the door.

"A cheerful heart is good medicine,
but a crushed spirit dries up the bones."

—PROVERBS 17:22 NIV

Compassion

. . . is the special quality of **Self Sacrifice** that ultimately sets apart the one who possesses the true *HEART of a Caregiver.*

Compassion is *LOVE* in action . . . It is the *passion* to make a difference . . . and the *choice* to *sacrifice* personal comfort and convenience in order to help relieve suffering.

It's not easy to be involved with other people's pain . . . often it gets messy and sometimes it brings you to tears as well. But your *Caring HEART* is willing to step over that line saying . . . *"I know this will be hard and it may hurt, but if it helps somebody else, it will be worth it all."*

You may get burned out and exhausted at times, but this is at the core of who you are and it permeates everything you do. It's what separates you from the crowd and makes you a *HERO.* You have made a *choice* to be involved and share the burden of pain in your world.

It's not just a job . . . it's a *Calling.* . . because you have a *Heart* that sincerely **CARES** for others.

"Fear grows out of the things we think;
It lives in our minds.

Compassion grows out of the things we are,
and lives in our HEARTS."

— Barbara Garrison

AS THE HEART OPENS...

by Paula J. Fox

The *Heart of a Caregiver* is a compassionate *HEART*... a heart that is wide open to experience the pain and heartache of others. Not everyone shares this ability to be so vulnerable and willing to participate in someone else's suffering in order to bring some relief.

In her book, *From the Heart Through the Hands*, Dawn Nelson describes an incident from her own experience that illustrates how we make a *CHOICE* to open our hearts to the pain and suffering of another. And when we make that choice... **as the Heart opens**... *COMPASSION* emerges and we are able to help.

"I listened as the woman sitting across from me spoke about how much she loved her husband and what a kind and decent man he was. She recalled the warm summer evening when he offered to walk to the corner grocery to pick up an item or two to complete their evening meal. In my mind's eye I could see her pick up the telephone when it rang.

The woman stopped speaking for a moment as tears welled in her eyes and began to roll down her face. She said that when she arrived at the hospital, her husband's body was unrecognizable. A speeding truck felled him just as he stepped off the curb.

As she re-lived those moments that so dramatically changed her life, I realized that her words were reaching my ears, yet I was not letting them into my HEART. I didn't want to experience her pain or to accept the possibility that such a thing could happen to me. In the same moment, I realized that unless I was willing to accept the possibility of my own suffering, I could not be truly PRESENT to receive hers.

*I made a decision to OPEN to this woman's sorrow. As I did so, my own tears began to flow and my heart began to ache. As I received her grief, it was as if **my mind visited her heart.** I felt the tiniest spark of what she felt and that moment gave birth to my **Compassion.**"*

As the HEART opens . . . COMPASSION overcomes fear and gives us the ability to focus on the needs of another and to offer whatever help is needed . . . regardless of the personal cost.

"Become so wrapped up in something
that you forget to be afraid."

— LADY BIRD JOHNSON

"If the world is going to be healed
through human efforts,
I am convinced it will be by ordinary
people ... people whose love for LIFE
is greater than their fear."

— Joanne Macy

This is a story that touched my heart.
My daughter-in-law was there to share both the
sorrow and the joy of this journey. . . bearing the
beautiful marks of Compassion. She described
it as one of "the hardest and yet most fulfilling"
experiences of her career as a nurse.

"By COMPASSION . . .

we make others' misery our own,

and so, by relieving them,

we relieve ourselves also."

— Thomas Brown, Sr.

CELEBRATION OF LIFE

by Paula J. Fox

It's never easy being involved . . . in someone else's pain
It's the hardest part that *Nurses* have to play
But they also have the privilege . . . of sharing special joys . . .
Blessings that can happen along the way

The setting was a delivery room . . . the tone was very sad
but this story will inspire you in the end
A birth that brought so many tears . . . but joyous ones as well
Let me tell you how it all began

Conceived in love and cherished . . . while he was yet unborn
His parents learned he had anencephaly
But this child was such a precious gift, they chose to give him *LIFE*
regardless of how short his days might be

They named their baby Benjamin . . . meaning *"Son of my right hand"*
because he was a special part of them
They took advantage of each day . . . to *celebrate his life*
knowing just how quickly it would end

The journey was still painful . . . but their story's one of *HOPE*
as their lives became an ***Inspiration*** to all
Hearts were touched . . . and Faith renewed . . . Trust in God restored
for the Doctors, Nurses, and others who were on call

The *LOVE* they shared for their unborn child was special to behold
And their *FAITH* encouraged many along the way
There was a birthday *celebration* . . . when Benjamin was born
For no one knew if he'd live to see that day

His parents prayed to have a chance . . . to hold him in their arms
even if for just a little while
To touch and feel his little face and kiss each tiny toe
To express their love and try to coax a smile

When he finally made his entrance . . . his lifeless body was blue
It looked like he had not survived his birth
But suddenly they heard him cough . . . and he began to *breathe*
as God gave him extra hours here on earth

The delivery room exploded into. . . *a Celebration of Life!*
What a miracle . . . this special little boy!
There were balloons and cake and photographs . . . as people filled
the room . . . Lots of tears and laughter and great *JOY!*

God gave his parents a gift that day . . . an experience they will treasure
priceless moments holding and loving their son
And all who shared the journey . . . felt privileged to be there
to *CELEBRATE the LIFE* of this precious one!

Family, friends and medical staff . . . who attended this *miracle birth*
will cherish the memory . . . so *blessed* to play a part
And the *Nurse* who held his mother's hand through her times of joy
and grief . . . still holds a special place for her in her ***HEART***.

"The gift of **LIFE**,
God's special gift,
is no less beautiful
when it is accompanied by
illness or weakness
or hunger, or poverty,
mental or physical handicaps,
loneliness, or old age.
Indeed, at these times,
human life gains extra splendor
as it requires our special
CARE, concern and

REVERENCE."

— Terence Cardinal Cooke

"LIVING WHILE DYING"

A Hospice Nurse's Story

by Marjorie Beth Henderson, RN, BSN, CHPN

Delicate and frail, the 90-year-old woman lay quietly in the hospital bed, her shallow breathing barely discernible. Silvery hair framed her kind face where velvety wrinkles had been caressed by many-a-grandchild, and remnants of laugh-lines marked the corners of her mouth.

Praying that this dear lady's family would arrive in time, I gently placed her fragile hand in mine. *"Miss Elly, I'm still here. I'm going to stay with you until your family comes."* Her eyelids flickered. Leaning forward, I caressed her hand and prayed that peace would prevail over pain and surpass all fear and unanswered questions.

In moments like this, nothing is more important than this one precious life and the passing that is taking place. Other pressing nursing duties fall away and priorities re-set themselves.

Without exception, the *hospice nurses* I know view their work as **not just a job, but a *Calling***. While at work, these nurses place their personal worlds of problems and cares on hold to focus on patients who have six months to live—or six hours. They zero-in on families who face multiple responsibilities and the inevitable void that the absence of this loved one will bring.

Hospice nurses strive to help patients and families *"put the pieces together"* as their world seems to be falling apart. Patients and families are encouraged to continue meaningful daily *LIVING,* assisted to complete necessary tasks at hand, and offered support as they ride the emotional roller coaster of acceptance, denial, and *LIFE.*

For hospice patients, death is a process and end-of-life care becomes a major determinant in what their *quality of LIFE* will be. One must understand that *the "dying process"* is on an uncertain timeline that falls into the realm of *"LIVING."*

In other words, we continue *"LIVING while Dying."*

*"The truth is, most dying people are still interested in the same things they were interested in before they knew they were dying. If he's an avid sports fan, that's not necessarily going to go away. If he cares about you, chances are he'll want to hear about what's happening in your life, just as he did before. Talking about daily life affirms the fact that, while his life is limited . . . **He's still LIVING!**"*

— Angela Morrow, RN

As a hospice nurse, my goal is to truly help each of my patients *"LIVE until they die"* . . . to provide *Compassionate CARE* that promotes the highest quality of *LIFE* possible until that last breath is taken. May the passing of each person be with *dignity*, in the circumstances of their choice.

And if at all possible—may there be at least one *Caring* person present to hold their hand.

"What an honor to provide for the
deepest human needs during illness,
both physiologically and psychologically...

To have the courage to help ill people LIVE, and
to have the courage to be there when they die...

To provide dignity and comfort... not only
to the patient, but to their loved ones as well."

— Michelle RN

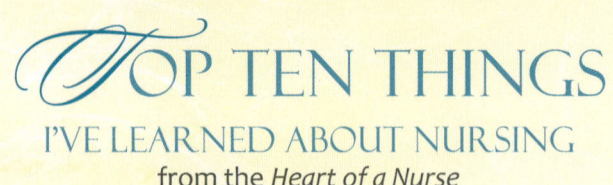

TOP TEN THINGS

I'VE LEARNED ABOUT NURSING

from the *Heart of a Nurse*

1. Nursing is the *hardest* and *easiest* thing I've ever done.

2. Our profession has no room for *bullies* or *whiners*.

3. The more unloving a patient acts, the more he *needs to be loved*.

4. It's usually better to *beg forgiveness* than to ask permission . . . especially if you're taking a St. Bernard to see a child in ICU.

5. A lot of patients get well in spite of us, but even more get well *because* of us.

6. Some things have to be *believed* to be seen.

7. *Healing the spirit* is as important as healing the mind.

8. Every day that I've *held a hand* but forgotten to chart vitals . . . I still may have come out ahead.

9. If I don't get *emotionally involved* with my patients . . . it's time for me to change professions.

10. If I can't cure, I can still **CARE**.

"CARING is the essence
of Nursing."

—Jean Watson, Ph.D., RN

> *"Occasionally in life there are those moments . . . which can only be articulated by the inaudible Language of the Heart."*
>
> — Martin Luther King, Jr.

THE LANGUAGE OF CARING

by Paula J. Fox

Actions speak softly to those in distress
like messages straight from the *HEART*
Without any words . . . it's the *Language* expressed
by those who make *CARING* an *ART*

It's the *Language of* heartfelt *EMPATHY*
that sees through another's eyes
Understanding the patient's feelings
giving *CARE* that is sensitive and wise

It's the *Language of* **COMFORT** that eases the pain
both the physical and emotional kind
Those who are hurting or suffer loss
need *CARE* for both body and mind

It's the *Language of* **PEACE** that offers relief
from anxiety . . . and despair
The *CARING* heart gives calm reassurance . . .
sometimes . . . by just *being there*

It's the *Language* of **KINDNESS** . . .
that *CARES* for each patient with dignity and respect
Touching the heart and soul of the person
finding little ways to connect

It's the *Language* expressed with a gentle **TOUCH**
to mend a body that's broken
It can also convey your genuine *CARE*
without a word being spoken

It's the *Language* of *silence* . . . that pauses to **LISTEN**
and communicates that you *hear*
Showing you *CARE* what others are feeling
builds trust and alleviates fear

It's the *Language* of constant **ENCOURAGEMENT**
in the battle to overcome pain
Your positive *CARE* can inspire others
to dance . . . in the midst of the rain

It's the *Language* of **JOY** and laughter
that helps the body to heal
When the *CARE* you give . . . lifts a patient's spirit
it reduces the pain they feel

It's the *Language* of **HOPE** from a heart that *CARES*
in the darkness . . . a bright ray of light
As you celebrate every small victory . . .
you give strength to continue the fight

It's the *Language* of great **COMPASSION**
always willing to sacrifice
It means *CARING* enough to share in the pain
paying a personal price

It's painful to watch others hurting so much
sometimes you can't help but cry
But this *HEART* makes a *choice* to be involved
to help people *live* . . . and die.

There's a *hero* in the *Heart of a Caregiver*
with courage and toughness too
Choosing to help means taking a risk
doing what others won't do

What a privilege to honor this Caregiver's *HEART*
that serves with such passion and daring
This world would be a much darker place
without the . . .

Language of Caring

"There is a

LIGHT

in this world, a healing
spirit more powerful
than any darkness we may
encounter. It will emerge
through the lives
of ordinary people who
hear a call and answer in
extraordinary ways."

— Mother Teresa

About the Author

Paula J. Fox describes herself as a lifetime student whose passion is to continue learning and applying godly wisdom in her life so that she can share it with others. Her desire is to inspire and motivate others to live a life of purpose and significance. She is a teacher at heart with a degree in special education and 35 years experience teaching and leading all ages from preschool through adult.

She and her husband, Larry, have three grown children, and she is now able to devote more of her time to writing. Besides being a teacher and leader in her own church, she is the founder and leader of L'dor (Ladies' day of renewal), a home-based Bible study for women. This ministry, which began over 25 years ago, meets weekly in homes where they worship together through songs and scriptures, sharing and studying God's Word together. Paula loves researching and writing her own lessons for L'dor as well as writing poetry and prose. She also enjoys speaking to women's groups and retreats.

Paula J. Fox is the author of several Simple Truths books including:

Heart of a Teacher
Mothers Are Heaven's Scent
The Second Mile

You may contact Paula J. Fox at: paulajfox@live.com

Satisfied customers are our #1 priority, so I encourage you to give us feedback on how we're doing. If we ever disappoint you, I hope you'll let us know, and we will do everything we can to make it right.

If you have enjoyed this book we invite you to check out our entire collection of gift books, with free inspirational movies, at www.simpletruths.com. You'll discover it's a great way to inspire friends and family, or to thank your best customers and employees.

For more information, please visit us at:

www.simpletruths.com or call us toll free... **800-900-3427**